Promote Yourself!

Wallace D. Wattles

The Cause of Success
is the Man
who Succeeds;
Something in
The Man has been
applied to his work,
and has produced
a certain result.

PROMOTE YOURSELF!

CREATING BUSINESS & PERSONAL
SUCCESS IN THE CERTAIN WAY

By

Wallace D. Wattles

Originally Published Posthumously in 1914

Author of the 1910 Classic
THE SCIENCE OF GETTING RICH

www.JonRosePublishing.com

Published by

JonRose
Publishing™

PMB 239
13 Summit Square Center
Langhorne, PA 19047-1098
800-582-4178
215-734-2288 fax
info@JonRosePublishing.com

PROMOTE YOURSELF!

by

Wallace D. Wattles

Originally published in 1914

JonRose Publishing - Innovative eBooks
for your Health, Education and Enjoyment.

TABLE OF CONTENTS

How to Make Connections

By the Original 1914 Publisher, Elizabeth Towne

THIS LITTLE BOOK IS A LIVE WIRE. Make the right connection with it and success is yours.

How shall you do it? By reading it long and often; by going back to it every time you catch your confidence and purpose ebbing; and by acting up to its teachings in every way you can think of.

The Life of all success is The Spirit of Faith and Good Will.

Whenever you feel your faith ebbing get back to this Live Wire again. Live with it until its spirit is yours and you recognize yourself as THE MAN WHO CAN.

Victory in Defeat

By Edwin Markham

Defeat may serve as well as victory
To shake the soul and let the glory out. When
the oak is straining in the wind.

The boughs drink in new beauty, and the
trunk Sends down a deeper root on the windward
side. Only the soul that knows the mighty grief

Can know the mighty rapture. Sorrows come
To stretch out spaces in the heart for joy.

CHAPTER 1
THE BUSINESS ATTITUDE

LIKE CAUSES, UNDER LIKE CONDITIONS, PRO-
DUCE LIKE EFFECTS; business success is an effect,
and cannot be an exception to the law of cause and
effect.

The cause of success is the man who succeeds;
something in the man has been applied to his work,
and has produced a certain result.

What is it in the man which produces the result of
success?

It is not physical strength, although physical
strength may be a great aid; all strong men do not
succeed, however, and those who do have the ability to so apply their physical strength as to make
it assist in producing the result of success.

It is not intellectual ability, for all intellectually able
men do not succeed; those who do have the power
to so direct their intellectual ability as to make it
assist in the achievement of success.

The potency which makes the successful man, therefore, is the power to so apply physical and mental ability as to produce results.

This power must be an attitude of the man himself. It is not a special gift to a few, nor is it a rudimentary faculty which each may develop; it is a position to be assumed. If his abilities and energies are to be directed, it is the man himself who must direct them; and if he directs them he is the potency which causes success.

Every man has the inherent power to direct his own abilities and energies; and every man is conscious of having this power. It is because he has it that he is capable of growth and progress. To make a successful man, it is necessary to make one who knows what things result in success, and who will direct his energies to do those things; and the first essential to this is that he should assume the attitude of self-direction.

Every man is either self-directing or directed by the suggestions which come from his environment. The man who can is always a self-directing man; the man who is directed by suggestion is the man who cannot.

The man who is directed by suggestion has a

"horoscope;" his destiny is decided by heredity and environment; the self-directing man does not allow his thoughts to be dictated by heredity, environment or the stars; he thinks what he wants to think, and if his' scope does not suit him he makes a better one.

Business success depends upon business policy; business policy can only be formulated by thought; therefore, whether a man succeeds or fails depends upon the way he thinks.

The directed man only thinks the thoughts which are suggested by his environment; and so he can only do what those around him think he can do.
The self-directing man thinks what he wants to think, and can therefore do what he wants to do.

To become the man who can, the first step is to take the attitude of self- direction.

Receive and consider every suggestion which comes from your environment, but do not act on the suggestion; act on your own conclusions about the suggestion.

Digest and assimilate suggestions as you digest and assimilate food; make them a part of your own thought before you use them, and learn to reject any that are indigestible.

CHAPTER 2
WHAT YOU DESIRE

SUCCESS IS BECOMING WHAT YOU WANT TO BE, and is obtained by applying your energies to your work; and you will apply your energies in exact proportion to the intensity of your desire, and to your faith in your ability to become what you want to be.

The intensity of your desire will depend on the clearness with which you picture to yourself what you want to be.

Vague and indefinite longings will never call out your best effort.

Form a mental picture of what you want to be, and of all that you want in person, property and environment; dwell upon it until it is clear and definite to you, and hold it until it arouses intense desire.

Think about this picture until you are always conscious of it, no matter what you may be doing, so that it is always in the background of your consciousness.

But even though you have strong desire you will not put forth your best effort without confidence; you will have to think you can before you can.

And you cannot think you can unless you feel that you can; and so you need to have demonstrated to you the fact that you cannot feel that you can unless you have within you the power that can.

In other words, if you strongly desire to do a thing, it is certain proof that you have the power to do it.

Desire is the result of feeling, and the feeling which results in desire is a faculty seeking expression.

The desire to sing or play music is the musical faculty seeking expression, and if there were no faculty, or power, there could be no desire. We cannot desire things which do not harmonize with the forces within, for a thing which does not harmonize with the forces within is repulsive to us. Things only harmonize with those of the same essential nature; therefore, if you desire a thing it is because that thing is essentially and potentially within you.

What is within you essentially must be within you potentially.

When we see a generous and sympathetic man we

desire to be like him because the sight arouses generosity and sympathy within us; and the power to be, seeking expression, causes the desire to be.

When we hear a great oration or a beautiful song, we desire to execute a similar performance because the faculties of oratory or music respond to the stimulus and seek expression.

Desire is a power seeking expression. You cannot desire what is not potentially within you; and therefore, you can be what you want to be.

The fact that you want to be is proof that you can be.

First, form a clear conception of what you want to be in person, property and environment; and then understand that in so far as your desires are not contrary to Eternal Justice it is absolutely certain that you can be what you want to be.

CHAPTER 3
BECOMING WHAT YOU WANT TO BE

SUCCESS IS A PROGRESSIVE EVOLUTION of the faculties of the successful man. To understand this, remember that success is becoming what you want to be; becoming what you want to be consists in satisfying your desires, and desire is the effort of a faculty to come into action.

Each gain in money or position that a man may make enables him to bring into use a new faculty, or to make fuller use of an old one; this satisfies desire, and is success.

The man who can use the most of his faculties is the man who can; and because he is the man who can, he is the successful man.

Success, then, being an evolution of the successful man, must follow the evolutionary principle of action; and the basic fact in evolution is that each lower plane contains all the potentialities required to perform the functions of the higher plane.

On ascending to a higher plane, new faculties are brought into use; but we also see the continued use of the faculties which were active on the lower plane; and it is the complete development of these faculties, or their fullest possible use which makes ascension to a higher plane possible.

Evolution never reaches the higher plane from imperfectly developed specimens on the lower plane, but always from the most perfectly developed.

In other words, it is the evolutionary principle that those organisms which function most perfectly on the lower plane are nearest to the higher plane; and the way to approach the higher plane is by perfecting function on the lower plane.

More than this is necessary, however, for if no organism ever did more than to function perfectly on its own plane there would be no evolution.

Evolution begins when organisms begin to add to the necessary functions of the plane on which they are living; calling into use faculties which can be perfected only on a higher plane.

Your present work may not be the work you want to do; but unless you can do your present work perfectly you are not ready for the work you want to do. And even when you can do your present work perfectly, if that is all that you can do you are not ready for anything else.

It is only when you can do your present work perfectly, and do some other work besides, that you are ready to advance.

Evolution is brought about by developing the faculties which are to be used on a higher plane; and this is done by first doing perfectly the work of the lower plane and then adding to it, so as to bring other faculties into use, or to so develop those already in use that they become too large to find expression on the lower plane.

To rise, you must not only fill your present place, but you must more than fill it: it is that part of you which projects beyond the boundaries of your present place which gets hold on the higher place.

The evolutionary principle of success is that you should more than fill your present place; and you can succeed in no other way.

CHAPTER 4
PROMOTING YOURSELF

THE SUCCESSFUL LIFE IS THE ADVANCING LIFE; and the advancing life is lived by obedience to the evolutionary principle. The evolutionary principle is that advancement comes by more than filling your present place; and this is true whether you are an employee or are in business for yourself.

However, a mere purposeless doing of more work than is required will not advance you; it will probably only tend to keep you where you are. If you are an employee and have no ambition but to more than fill your present place, it will be to your employer's interest to keep you in your present place; and he will probably do so. You must know what you want to be, and you must more than fill your present place for the purpose of becoming what you want to be.

Do not do extra work with the idea that by so doing you may curry favor with your employer; that will put you in a servile attitude, and out of the attitude of self-direction.

Do not do it in the hope that those above you will

see your good service and promote you; they may find it more profitable to keep you where you are.

Do what you do with the purpose of promoting yourself. You are more than filling your place in order to develop your faculties for filling a larger place; if your employer does not offer you one when you are ready for it, offer yourself to another employer.

There are always places for the Advancing Man.

Keep your mind fixed on what you want to be, and more than fill your present place; your mental attitude will make you quick to see every opportunity for bettering your condition, and you will be competent to take advantage of opportunities when they come.

Do not wait for an opportunity to be all that you want to be; be all that you can today, and when an opportunity to be more is offered to you, take it.

There is no such thing as lack of opportunities for the man who is living the advancing life, and who has an advancing mind.

Everything that touches your life is an opportunity, if you discover its proper use.

Every circumstance, every seeming misfortune, every person you meet, every dog that barks at you, or wags his tail as you pass—all have some element of usefulness to you if you will find it. Study them all, for they are your opportunities. Most men fail by waiting for some particular kind of opportunity, instead of being ready to seize every opportunity.

Steadily hold the picture of all that you want to attain in person, property and environment; live the advancing life within, by more than filling your present place; live the accumulative life without, by acquiring everything you meet which belongs in your picture, and you cannot fail. The stars in their courses will fight for you; your success will be made by the evolutionary principle, the creative power of the universe.

CHAPTER 5
THE ADVANCING THOUGHT

IF YOU ARE IN BUSINESS FOR YOURSELF, the evolutionary principle of success is the same as if you were working for another. You must keep in mind what you want to become, and more than fill your present place each day.

That does not mean that you are to try to do part of tomorrow's work today. You have nothing to do with tomorrow's work, except to be ready for it when it comes; but you must do all that is necessary for today's business, and something for increase. In every transaction you must keep the advancing mind; you must put the expanding thought into everything you do, and communicate it to every person with whom you have dealings.

If you sell a pound of sugar, do it with the thought that the purchaser's trade is valuable because he will soon be able to buy in barrel lots; if a child buys a penny's worth of candy, put into the sale the thought that he will one day buy a five-pound box; and in each case see that the customer gets the thought.

Put into every sale the thought of advance for the customer as well as for yourself; soon they will all feel that they are getting bargains in everything. And they will be right.

If you thus put the advancing thought into every transaction, your customers will get it in regard to their own affairs; and they will begin to be more successful and will mentally connect their success with you.

This will strongly attract them to you; the best bargain you can give a man is to communicate to him the advancing thought in regard to his own affairs. No "premium" or "rebate" is equal to it.

When you send a man away feeling that he is advancing, and becoming a more valuable customer, you give him the strongest possible inducement to visit you again.

If you communicate the advancing thought to your customers, they will begin to make successes because of it; and intuitively connecting their successes with you, will come to you for more power. You will build them up, and they, in turn, will build you up.

The man who can give the advancing thought to

all who deal with him cannot fail; he has exactly what they are seeking.

This principle holds good whether you are a merchant, an artist, a professional man, actor, singer — no matter what. You can more than fill your present place; so that your customers, patrons or audiences will know that they are getting a bargain.

It is not the quantity or quality of the goods that makes the bargain; it is the feeling of advancement, or increase.

The basic element of success in business is, therefore, to hold the thought and the mental attitude of advancement; and to more than fill your present place.

And you more than fill your place by so doing your work that those who deal with you are conscious of being advanced by you.

By study and application of the evolutionary principle, success is made a certainty, and failure rendered impossible.

CHAPTER 6
THE LAW OF OPULENCE

*"Except a man be born again he cannot see
the kingdom of God."*

IN LIVING THE NEW LIFE THE FIRST ESSEN-
TIAL is to abandon the idea of competition and of
a limited supply. Too many people who consider
themselves practitioners of the new thought never entirely succeed in doing this.

Competition in business originates in the idea of a
limited supply. It grows out of the supposition that
because there is not enough to go round, men must
compete with each other for what there is.

Many people who have a partial grasp of the new
thought still suppose that it is necessary that
some should be poor in order that others may
have enough, and believe that wealth is possible
only to those who have superior ability, or the
power to attract to themselves a larger portion
from the limited supply.

These people try to apply the new thought princi-
ples on the competitive plane, and they do so with a
fair degree of success; they try to develop a superior

attracting power; they inject new motives and new energy into competitive business methods; they assert, "I am success," all the while believing that they can succeed only because ninety-five per cent of all others fail.

The majority of these competitive new thought people do achieve a great measure of success because their faith gives them just the energy, push and optimism which are necessary in competitive business. The confidence born of their belief makes a majority of their actions successful actions; their partial application of new thought ideas makes them exceptionally able competitors, and they attribute their success to thought-power and to affirmation when it is almost purely competitive.

But this kind of so-called new thought is really only the highest and most fully perfected form of the old thought. It only sees Caesar's kingdom after all; it has no conception of the kingdom of God.

All the final results show that these new thought people are only a part of Caesar's kingdom. Their fortunes fluctuate. They meet with losses and their business suffers from panics. Their prosperity is checkered by periods of adversity. Their sense of safety is mere self-confidence; deep in the subconscious they always carry the germ of secret fear.

No one can ever be wholly free from fear who recognizes any limitation in the supply, for if there is not enough to go round, we know that our turn to go without may come at any time.

The lapses and failures of new thought people are traceable directly to the idea of a limited supply; to the idea that success and the attainment of wealth are possible only to a part of us.

Is there any truth in this idea that competition is necessary? Let us see.

The things that are essential to life and advancement, mental and physical, may be roughly grouped under five heads, and these are: Food, clothing, shelter, education and amusement. For three of these— food, clothing and shelter—we look to the world of nature for supply. These three—with their appurtenances and extensions in the way of luxuries, decorations, art and beauty—constitute what we call wealth.

Is there any limitation to the supply of these?

Take into consideration, first, the question of food supply. In this country we have not yet begun to sound the possibilities of intensive agriculture, making four blades of grass grow where one grew before.

It is a fact capable of mathematical demonstration that the single state of Texas, if all its resources were organized for the production of food, would produce enough to feed the whole present population of the globe, and feed them well.

Our food products range from wheat in the Dakotas to rice in Carolina; from northern fruits in Michigan to oranges in California and Florida. This country alone, intensely cultivated, would feed the inhabitants of ten worlds like this. There is no lack in the food supply.

When we pray to our Father, "Give us our daily bread," we should never forget to add a thanksgiving that He already answered that prayer when He laid the foundation of the world.

Remember, too, that the work of men like Burbank has just begun; the food supply is capable of infinite development. There is, therefore, no need for men to compete with each other in order to get enough to eat.

As to the second essential, clothing, we find the same to be true.

The United States can produce cotton for the world, but it is not necessary to dress the world in anything so cheap as cotton fabrics. We have sheep ranges to supply the woolen goods for all, and fields in which to raise the flax for fine linen; there are great wastes of land, now barren, where we might grow enough mulberry trees to feed the silk worms necessary to clothe the world in silks; we even have the deserts on which to raise ostriches for fine plumage. We have resources sufficient to clothe every man, woman and child in raiment finer than that of Solomon in all his glory. And there are undreamed of possibilities in the despised weeds by the wayside; some Burbank will presently develop them into the raw material for fabrics more beautiful than the world has ever seen.

The supply of clothing is inexhaustible. No need to compete with another here; no need for one to go in sackcloth that another may wear purple and fine linen; there is purple and fine linen for all.

Taking up the question of shelter we find the same conditions prevailing. There are great banks of clay waiting to be made into bricks and tile; there are vast ledges of building stone unquarried as yet; we have learned that brick may be made of sand and lime, and that cement is excellent building material.

It is an indisputable fact that a mansion finer than Vanderbilt's might be erected for every family in

America, and when all were finished we should hardly have made a scratch on the surface of our supply of building material. No need for some to live in hovels in order that others may be delicately housed!

And the supply for interior furnishings—for furniture, carpets, books, musical instruments, pictures, statuary, everything to delight the eye and mind of man is just as unlimited.

Truly, there is no scarcity of things; nor is there any lack of work that ought to be done. There is no necessity in nature for competition, either for things or for jobs. There is enough useful and beautiful work waiting to be done to keep us all busy all our lives.

And it may be well to point out here that there is no lack in the supply of finished products because labor is not productive enough to keep pace with the demand. Modern machinery has solved the problem of production. The producing power of labor has been multiplied by six hundred in a little more than a generation. In making nails, for instance, one man does the work which required a thousand men one hundred years ago; and the same is approximately true in all lines of industry; and the end of the increase in producing power is not yet.

There is nothing in which further improvement is not possible. Six hours' work a day, by all of us, would produce all that we could use, including every known luxury.

With such abundance in the whole, we do not need to compete for a part; we do not need to take thought for tomorrow; we do not need to experience panics or reverses.

We need only to seek for the kingdom of God, and His righteous relations toward each other, and all these things shall be added unto us.

And what is the kingdom of God?

CHAPTER 7
TO TRANSMUTE COMPETITION

*"Whereunto shall I liken the kingdom of God? It is like leaven,
which a woman took and hid in three measures of meal,
until the whole was leavened."*

THE KINGDOM OF GOD IS IN NATURE like the leaven in the meal—in all and through all. It includes all nature, for God is the cause of nature; and when nature is perfectly natural, there is the kingdom of God in all its fullness.

If God be the Mind of nature, then there can be no more perfect expression of God than in the naturalness of nature.

The kingdom of God includes all life, for God is the Life itself; and when life is lived in a perfectly natural way, there is the kingdom of God in all its fullness; for there can be no more perfect expression of God than the living of life in a natural way.

And this brings us to the question, how may life be lived in the natural way?

The living of life consists in continually advancing into more life.

Drop a seed in the center of a field; the life in the seed at once becomes active; it ceases to merely exist, and begins to live. Soon it produces a plant, and a seed head, in which there are thirty, sixty or a hundred seeds, each containing as much life as the first seed contained.

These fall into the ground, and in their turn begin to live; and in time there are a million seeds in the field, each containing as much life as the first seed contained.

The life of the first seed, by the mere act of living, has increased a million fold.

The living of life consists in continuously increasing life; there is no other way to live.

This necessity of life for increase is the cause of what we know as evolution.

There is no such thing as evolution in the mineral world. Minerals do not advance or progress. Lead does not evolve into tin, tin into iron, iron into silver, silver into gold, and so on.

Evolution is found only in the organic forms of life, and is caused by the natural necessity of life to find fuller and fuller expression.

Life on this earth began no doubt, in a single cell; but a single cell could not give sufficient expression to life, and so it formed a double celled organism; then organisms of many cells; then vertebrates; then mammals, and finally, man.

All this because of the inherent necessity of life to advance forever into more complete expression.

And evolution did not cease with the formation of man; physical evolution ceased, and mental and spiritual evolution began.

Man, from the beginning, has been developing more ability to live.

Each generation is capable of living more than the preceding generation. The race is continually advancing into more life, and so we see that the living of life means to live more.

The action of consciousness continually expands consciousness.

The primal necessity of mind is to know more, and feel more, and enjoy more; and this necessity of mind is the cause of social evolution, and of all progress.

35

If we take conscious life—as we must—to be the highest expression of God, or of the Mind of nature, then the purpose of all things must be to further the development of conscious life; and if man is the highest form of conscious life—and he is—then the purpose of all things must be to further the development of man.

And if the development of man consists in the increase of his capacity for life, then the purpose of all things in nature must be to further the continuous advancement of man into more and more of life.

Life finds expression by the use of things.

The measure of a man's life is not the things he possesses, but the number of things he is able to use rightly; and to have fullness of life is to have all the things we are capable of using rightly. The purpose of the Mind of nature being the continuous advancement of man into more life, it must also be the intention of that Mind that every man shall have the unrestricted use of all the things that he is capable of using and enjoying rightly; or that "his own shall come to him."

The purpose of God is that all should have life, and have it more abundantly.

God is the Mind of nature, and God is in all, and through all; therefore, the mind, or intelligence of God is in all and through all, like the leaven in the meal.

The desire for advancement is a fundamental fact in the action of mind; therefore, the desire for advancement is in all, and through all.

All things desire the advancement of every man.

If a man desires any good thing in order to live his life more fully, that thing desires him also.

The mind of things responds to the mind of man, when man desires advancement. All things work together for good to those who desire only advancement.

The greatest of all facts to us is the fact that there is a Mind in nature which desires us to have all the things we are capable of using, and willing to use, in the direction of fuller life, and that this Mind is in the things themselves, tending to bring them toward us; and that if we take the right course, recognizing this Mind and working with it, all things must come to us.

But this Mind is the Mind of the Whole, not of a

part; and if we lose sight of the Whole and enter into competition with our fellows for a part we lose all.

For competition of a part is virtually a denial and rejection of the Whole. He who recognizes and accepts the whole cannot compete for a part. It is the idea of competition for a limited supply which prevents us from seeing and accepting the Abundance which is ours. We still keep up the foolish struggle of Caesar's kingdom, because we cannot see the kingdom of God, which is all around us and within us.

"If my kingdom were of this world, then would my servants fight," said Jesus. We do not get fully out of the ideas of the kingdoms of this world; we still do more or less fighting.

But how are we to avoid competition, when the whole business world is proceeding on the method of competing for a limited supply? How can we get work without competing for jobs? Can we succeed in a competitive world without competing? Shall we withdraw from the world, and form communistic societies?

Certainly not. To try that is to fail. A communistic society is a body of people who do not compete with each other, but who do compete with everybody else.

No community can be complete unto itself without greatly limiting its members in the means of life; and to do this is to defeat the end aimed at.

And if it is not complete in itself, satisfying all its wants, it must compete with the outside world for what is lacking, and this is what we seek to avoid.

No separation of a part from the Whole in any way, will solve the problem. The community scheme is inconvenient, unnatural and impracticable.

Shall we establish socialism and the cooperative commonwealth?

We cannot do it, because socialism and the cooperative commonwealth can never be established; it must establish itself, and it may take it a long time yet to do so.

We cannot do away with competition by legislative enactment of any kind so long as the majority of men believe in the limited supply; so we must keep right on in business under the present system, and yet cease to compete.

Can we do it? Yes. But how?

CHAPTER 8
MAN AND MONEY

"I am come that they might have life;
and that they might have it more abundantly."

GOD, THE MIND OF NATURE, produces the Abundance of nature with the purpose of providing for the development of man; not of some men, but of man. The purpose of nature is the continuous advancement of life; and as man is the embodiment of God and the highest form of life, the purpose of nature must be the continuous advancement of every man into more abundant life.

That which seeks the advancement of every man cannot take anything from any man; therefore to be one with the Mind of nature is to seek the advancement of all at the expense of none; to seek to get for all what one desires to get for oneself.

This must lift one entirely out of the competitive thought. "What I want for myself, I want for all;" that is the declaration of independence aimed at the competitive system.

"Our" Father, give "us," that is the prayer of the advancing life. This declaration and prayer are in uni-

son with the Mind of nature; the man who so de-
clares and so prays is mentally one with all that
lives, God, nature and man; and this is the at-one-
ment.

To be mentally one with the Mind of things makes
you able to register your thoughts on that mind, and
your desires as well.

When you desire a thing, and your mind and the
Mind of things are one, that thing will desire you,
and will move toward you. If you desire dollars,
and your mind is one with the Mind that pervades
dollars and all things else, dollars will be permeated
with the desire to come to you, and they will
move toward you, impelled by the Eternal Power
which makes for more abundant life.

To obtain what you want, you only need to establish your own at-one-ment with the Mind of things,
and they will be drawn toward you.

But the primal purpose of the Mind of things is
the continuous advancement of ALL into more
abundant life; therefore, nothing will be taken
away from any man or woman and given to you
unless you give to that person more in the way of
life than you take away.

It will be plainly seen that the Divine Mind cannot be brought into action in the field of purely competitive business. God cannot be divided against Himself. He cannot be made to take from one and give to another. He will not decrease one man's opportunity to advance in life in order to increase another man's opportunity to advance in life. He is no respecter of persons, and has no favorites.

He is equally in all, equally for all, and at the service of all alike.

To make the at-one-ment, you must see that your business gives to all who deal with you a full equivalent in life for the money value of what you take from them.

I say in life; that does not necessarily mean in money value. Here is what many critics of the profit system fail to understand: that a thing of small value to one man may be of inestimable value to another who can use it for the advancement of life. A box of matches would be worth more to an Esquimaux than Millet's "Man with the hoe."

The value of a thing to a man is determined by the plane of life on which he stands: what is of no value on one plane, or in one stage of his development, is indispensable on another plane, or in another stage.

The life-giving power of any article may be out of all proportion to its monetary value. This book is not worth a dollar in so far as the cash value of the paper and ink are concerned, but one sentence in it may be worth thousands of dollars to any reader. You may sell an article for more than it cost you, making a profit; but the purchaser may put it to such use that it will be worth hundreds of times its cost to him, and in that case profit is no robbery. See that your business meets this fundamental requirement; that is the first step.

When you have done this you are one with that Intelligence in nature which is working for more life for all; you are "working together with Him," as St. Paul says; you and your Father are one. The aim of your work is that all may have life, and have it more abundantly.

What you seek for yourself you are seeking for all, and the mental principle in everything that you need begins to gravitate toward you. If you need dollars, the Mind of things IN the dollars is conscious of the need; and you can affirm with truth "Dollars want me." Dollars will begin to move toward you, and they will come, invariably, from those who need what you can give in exchange. The Divine Mind will attend to the transference of that which is needed for the advancement of life to the place where need exists.

This will apply not only to all that you need to keep your business going, but to all that you are capable of using to enter into fuller life yourself.

No good thing will be withheld from you.

Your unity with the Evolutionary Power, with the Purpose of nature, will be such that you will receive all that nature has to give. Because you will do always the will of God, all things are yours, and you need to compete with no one.

But you must bear in mind that your wants are impressed on the Divine Mind only by your faith. A doubt cuts the connection. Anxiety and fear cut the connection.

Exactly as you are in the matter of impressing your own subconscious mind, so you are in the matter of impressing the Mind of things.

Your affirmations fall flat unless they are made with the dynamic power of absolute faith.

The Mind of things will not act positively for doubt and hesitancy.

"Whatsoever things ye desire when ye pray, believe that ye receive them and ye shall have them."

We cannot walk and work with God and distrust Him at the same time. If you feel distrust, you impress the Mind of things with distrust of you, and things will move away from you rather than toward you.

The requirements for non-competitive success are very simple: First, desire for everybody what you desire for yourself, and be sure to take nothing from anybody without giving a full equivalent in life; and the more you give the better for you.

Then move out in the absolute faith that all you need for the fullest life you are capable of living will come to you.

Pray with unfaltering faith to the Father that it shall come to you, and thank Him in every prayer, from a heart full of gratitude that it DOES come to you.

Everything that comes to you then will mean more life to someone else.

Each gain you make will add to the wealth of someone else. What you get for yourself—life—you get for all.

Your success adds to the life, health, wealth and happiness of all. But someone says: Wherein does this differ from competition, after all? Are you not still competing with those in the same line of business? No! What you gain will not come from the limited supply for which others are struggling, but from the Whole.

Let me illustrate: It may be said that there is only a limited supply of money in the country; not enough to supply the needs of all.

Suppose a large number of people enter this Way of Life, and dollars begin to move toward them all, there will not be enough to go around. That is true, but the thought of need impressed upon the mind of things would react upon the minds of men; new currency laws would be passed; the bullion would begin to move toward the mints; and the printing presses to turn out bank notes if they were necessary to the advancement of life.

The Mind of things reaches beyond the coined cash, into the gold and silver lying in the hearts of the hills; and it will all begin to move forward when it is called for by the prayer of faith.

And the same is true of everything else. Not only the mints, but the mills will start whenever a sufficient number of people have entered the way of the Advancing life.

If it be urged that the wage system prevents the workers from living full lives, the answer is that whenever the workers begin to live full lives, if the wage system stands in the way of their advancement it will be changed. Their demand for more life will be all that is required to change it.

Life cannot be advanced by changing systems, but systems may be changed by the advance of life.

There is plenty of work to be done in the erection of useful and beautiful things; all that is needed is a demand for those things by those whose sole purpose is to use them to give more life to all.

As the number of such people increases, the prosperity of all will increase, and a constantly increasing proportion of all classes will come into the Truth, abandoning competition and the way of the limited supply, until the kingdom will be established on earth as it is in Heaven.

"And God shall wipe away all tears from their eyes; and there shall be no more crying, neither shall there be any more pain, and there shall be no night there."

CHAPTER 9
TALK THAT BUILDS

DO NOT TALK ABOUT POVERTY. It adds nothing to the wealth and happiness of the world to disseminate the information that you have always been poor, and have had a mighty hard struggle to get along. Poverty is no more a thing to boast of than ignorance is a thing to boast of. The old saying that it is no disgrace to be poor is only a half truth; in the true sense it is really a disgrace to be poor.

Nobody is poor, or having a hard struggle but (a) the ignorant, (b) the lazy, and (c) the incompetent.

This sounds harsh, and you are ready to go "up in the air" about it; you want to tell me that the tenement dwellers and wage-slaves have no chance, and so on.

But wait a little. The wage slaves really own the world; they have created it all, and they could take possession of it tomorrow if they would. They can begin, at any time, to use the factories to make things for themselves, instead of turning wealth out for their masters.

But they do not do it because they are (a) too ignorant to know that this is their world; (b) too intellectually lazy to THINK, and so discover that this is
their world; and (c) incompetent, because they do
not THINK.

Intellectual laziness is what keeps the masses down;
those who work hard and willingly in other ways
shrink from the effort of sustained and consecutive
thinking; and because they let other people do their
thinking for them, they are slaves.

The masses will be wage-slaves as long as the five-
cent theaters are crowded and the public libraries
deserted.

I tell you this because I want to make plain to you
the futility of talking about poverty. Talking about
poverty and adverse conditions will only lead
people to run to the cheap shows, and to try in
other ways to drown their miseries in temporary
pleasures.

The more you talk, and think about your hard times,
the more you will be inclined to seek some mental
narcotic to dull the keen edge of your suffering; and
the longer you will suffer.

No surer way to keep the masses poor can be devised than to continually write and talk about their poverty.

Talk about the good time coming.

The good time IS coming, and the rapidity of its coming is in exact proportion of the number of people who think about it and talk about it.

Instead of going about showing horrible pictures of the condition of those who live in the tenements, go about showing beautiful pictures of the conditions of those who will live in the coming city.

If you can inspire one person to go to work for the coming city, you have done more good than you can by sending ten people out with slaves and plasterers to relieve existing distress.

Instead of crusading against child labor and bad factory conditions, tell the working people what splendid conditions they will have when they wake up and begin to operate the industries for themselves.

The masses are not in bondage to anything but ignorance and intellectual laziness; they can have what they will if they will begin to THINK.

And the way to make them think is to talk

WEALTH. That is the philosophy for the mass.

And the same applies to you as an individual.

If the mass is not ready or willing to rise, you do not have to stay down with it; you can rise above it.

But you can never rise above it if you keep talking about yourself as being down with it.

If you keep talking of yourself as one of those who have hard times in getting along, you will continue to be one of those who have hard times in getting along.

Do not tell how poor your parents were, and what terrible times you had when you were a child. To talk of those things is to go back into those conditions, mentally; and to go back into those conditions mentally is to invite them physically.

Talk about the happy times you had in your youth, and forget all the unhappy times.

Do not tell how hard you used to work, and how little you got for it. If you worked hard for nothing, you were a chump; and you should not advertise yourself as a chump.

Tell of the good work you have done, and of the good wages you got for it; then you are advertising yourself as a competent person, who can earn good wages.

Do not, like Uriah Heep, tell how 'umble you are, and boast of living in a 'umble abode, declare yourself to be as good as the best, and describe the elegant home you are in the process of getting and furnishing. Don't apologize for your clothes, tell how few you have, or say you "have nothing fit to wear;" think of the fine clothes you are making arrangements to get.

Don't talk poverty in any way; don't refer to it as existing.

TALK WEALTH.

PROMOTE YOURSELF!
Proudly brought to you by
JonRose Publishing

www.JonRosePublishing.com

Other titles available from JonRose Publishing

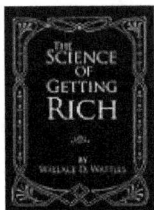

The Science of Getting Rich
by Wallace D. Wattles

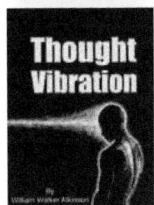

Thought Vibration
By William Walker Atkinson

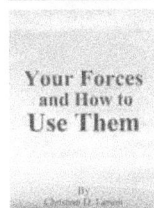

Your Forces and How to Use Them
by Christian D. Larson

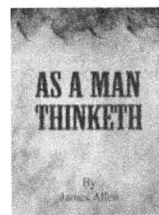

As A Man Thinketh
by James Allen

The Law of Success in Sixteen Lessons
by Napoleon Hill

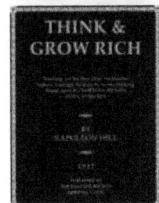

Think and Grow Rich
by Napoleon Hill

www.ingramcontent.com/pod-product-compliance
Lightning Source LLC
Chambersburg PA
CBHW060720030426
42337CB00017B/2934